The Mountain and the Pebble
the philosophy of, the art of, photography

David A. Melges

Copyright © 2013 David A. Melges
All rights reserved.
ISBN: 1493759523
ISBN-13: 978-1493759521

For anyone...

who has wanted to become their own,
unique and separate,

artist.

1.

A young boy wanted most to be a great photographic artist. So he went to study with a great photographer.

The first day the student brought two pictures to the great photographer and said "which is better?"

The expert pointed to one, and the student learned from that.

The next day the student brought 5 pictures to the great photographer and said "which is best?"

The expert pointed to one, and the student learned from that.

Each day for years, the student brought his work to the great photographer and asked which is best.

Each day the expert chose which he thought was best, and the student learned.

After 10 years, the student had learned well, and had become just like the great photographer.

And therefore was not an artist, at all.

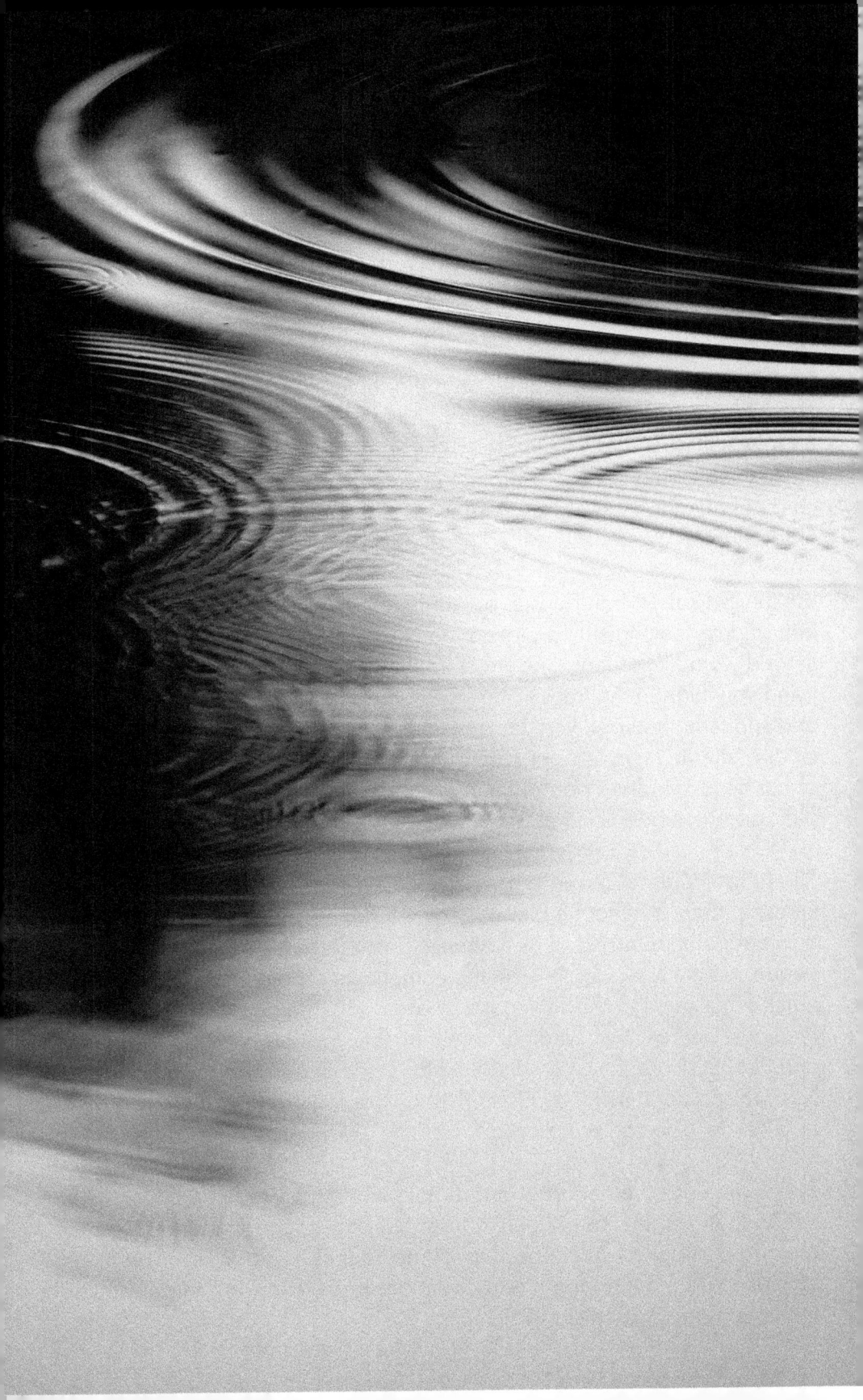

2.

A young girl said hello to an older woman working in her beautiful yard. Then asked "I see you have a brilliant red cardinal flying about, would it be ok if I took it's picture?"

The old woman said "I'd love to have you visit, and you're welcome to try, but I've chased that cardinal 'round my yard for years, you'll never get close enough for a picture.

The girl just smiled, and leaned on a tree at the edge of the yard. She watched the cardinal for the longest time, more than an hour, tracing it's path, watching it move from branch to branch to ground to branch. After a time, she chose a spot, close to the middle of yard, facing a branch the cardinal often landed on, but far far too close to it for the cardinal not to flare.

But the girl sat on the ground, pointed her camera at the branch, focused, adjusted her settings, then placed the camera in her lap. Then she watched the old woman garden. She watched the ants bustling, and the Orioles flying very high in the trees. She watched a bee move from flower to flower, and spotted a squirrel, very far down the lane running from tree to tree. Finally, after a very pleasant several hours, the cardinal had come to think of her as just another part of the yard, forgetting entirely that she was a girl...and he landed on her branch.

The girl still did not move, but waited for the cardinal to continue his path, knowing that now that he thought it was safe, it was only a matter of minutes before he returned to his favorite spot. Once he was in flight, she began, painfully slowly, to raise the camera, and point it at the branch. A quick adjustment to the settings to accomodate the change in sun, and then, just on cue, Mr. Cardinal came to rest...for only a moment...on the one PERFECT branch. With the PERFECT background, in the PERFECT soft light, raised up at just the PERFECT angle for the girl to capture one PERFECT shot. The camera clicked..................once.

She came back the next day, and the old woman invited her in for lemonade. Inside, the girl pulled from her bag a tube, and from the tube a rolled photograph...a large print of the PERFECT Cardinal. The older woman stared at it a long time with an amazed smile, and said "You know... in the backyard we have this Bluejay...."

Great photographers find beauty where others don't

Make beauty where apparently none exists

And capture beauty in ways others can't imagine

-dm

Two students of photography were given the assignment to create 12 photographs, with as much variety as possible.

When they returned, the first student had images of flowers, and the sky, and people and architecture and many other things, but student number two had taken 12 photos, all of water drops on blades of grass.

The instructor looked over both sets, and finally told the second student that he had passed, and could move on, and kindly asked the first student to retake the test.

Puzzled, the first student said "I don't understand, my photos clearly demonstrated the requirement of the challenge, every image was of a different subject, while the other student presented you with a series that was exactly the opposite of what you asked for."

The Master said "You brought me 12 photos of beautiful subjects, well photographed. But you should understand that in every case the subject was in the center, and the subject was the only thing of interest in the shot. In every case the photograph was from eye level, with the light behind you. You brought 12 of the EXACT SAME PHOTOGRAPH, merely changing the subject.

The other student, though I admit it took me a while to appreciate this, brought me 12 VERY different images, where the composition and style and technique changed with every one.

4.

For a change of pace, the instructor asked two students to follow along and watch another photographer at work, for several hours one afternoon.

Afterwards, the instructor asked each what they thought of the photographs...
...the first said "How can we know? We haven't seen them."

But the second student said "They're boring."

The instructor smiled and of course asked "How can you know?"

o which the student responded "He used only one lens, 50mm, or the focal length most like human vision...he shot everything on a tripod at eye level, meaning every shot looked exactly as we'd see it in real life. He could have been shooting at any time of day, but chose the point when the sun was highest, so the light wouldn't have been interesting, and photographed only the most obvious subjects on the path."

"He missed out on all the tools that he could have used to make photographs more interesting than seeing in real life."

The teacher was still smiling.

If you start off convinced that the square hole is round,

no amount of reasoning

will convince you to try to put the square peg in it.

-dm

I was at the park one day, about 5 years ago, shooting flowers. I happened to notice over yonder, a mother and daughter playing. Mom was trying to teach her 4 year old how to skip...it was pretty darned cute, woulda made a great picture.

After a while, the mom dragged a bike with training wheels out of the trunk of the car, and she chased after her little girl on that bike.....I kept thinking how, with a really long lens, I could get a great picture out of that....

Soon, mom pulled some sidewalk chalk out her bag, and the two of them drew HUGE flowers on the pavement.....I thought to myself how I could use a fisheye lens to get above them, and exaggerate the flowers stretching into the distance.
One of my favorite moments, pretty much ignoring my wildflowers now, was when the mom tried to jumprope with the hula hoop, failed, crashed and the daughter laughed hysterically......as a photographer one of my skills is to KNOW what would be a great picture, and THAT would be a great picture.

Mom laid on the ground, daughter sprinkled weeds all over her, GREAT picture.

They sang some silly song together, daughter on mom's lap, GREAT picture. The daughter fell down, Mom held her...........................GREAT picture.

After almost an hour of playing hard, the daughter got tired, and they both laid down on the grass.....the daughter picked a tiny flower and held it so close to Mom's eyes that Mom went cross-eyed looking at it.
Amazing picture.

You see a professional photographer knows their equipment...they know light, and composition, and they know angles and backgrounds. And very importantly, they know how to recognize a good picture when they see one.

cont.

But here's the irony of the story. This all took place in the hour AFTER I did a paid shoot for this mother and daughter. When they first got there I asked "What do you wanna do," Mom said "I don't know, you're the photographer."

I set them up in some normal, cute pictures, and asked again, "What do you wanna do?" Mom said, I'm not the creative one, I dunno."
We walked around, took some more ordinary, cute pictures, I gave them some suggestions, we took some more, then I asked "What do you wanna do?" Mom said "I dunno, stand in front of that tree?   Stand in front of that wall? Stand over by the water?"   I said "We can do that, but what's REALLY important, is what you're going to DO."

Mom said:

"I don't know what looks good in pictures."
"I'm not very creative."
"You're the photographer."
"I dunno."

After a while, I knew we had plenty of cute pictures, although nothing that really showed this mother and daughter being THEMSELVES. But they would be good pictures, so we called it "done" and I went off to shoot flowers.

And here's the lesson: If you let a photographer tell you how to be YOU, you're cheating yourself. A good photographer does NOT take over the shoot and boss you around and do your thinking for you.....they don't "invent" you.   They know their camera, they know the light, the angles, the backgrounds, and they can give you hints, and modify things you DO to make them more photogenic, but THEY CAN'T TELL YOU HOW TO HAVE FUN. They can't tell you HOW TO INTERACT WITH YOUR CHILD. THEY CAN'T TELL YOU HOW TO BE YOU.....they can't do those things and NOT cheat you.

1000 times this year, I'll struggle with customers trying to force them to decide WHAT TO DO. It's easy for me to just tell them....it saves me time....saves a LOT of frustration, because when you hear "I dunno you're the photographer" for the 5000th time you want scream, lol........but if I'm going to do a good job PHOTOGRAPHING YOU, I can't cheat you out of the opportunity to

BE YOU.

6.

As a final test, the student was handed a map to the great waterfall.

So stunningly beautiful a sight, so perfect yet natural. Surrounded by rain forest vegetation, pouring over jagged, jet black rocks, brilliant wildflowers, shafts of light caught in the mist, water of gold and blue...even the composition of the falls and the surrounding mountainside was perfect in its asymetry. All by itself the absolutely PERFECT image.

But getting there would be hard. The photographer would have to carry a heavy pack, for it takes 12 long days, hiking into the hills, and then the mountains. The terrain was hard, demanding, challenging, dangerous. The weather would alternate from scalding hot to bitter cold, and the student must endure.

Finally, after those 12 long days, he arrives at the waterfall. Looking at it, appreciating it, marveling. Perhaps no more beautiful a site in the world....

Magical.

And after years of training, and the arduous hike into the mountains, the student had earned the opportunity to...

...ignore the waterfall entirely. And challenge himself to make great photographs from the ordinary objects he found on his return trip.

Because he now finally understood, that ANYONE could take a picture of the waterfall....but the waterfall would deserve all the credit. Only an artist, strongest of will...

...could ignore it.

7.

At a point where I used to cross into a wooded area to take pictures, there was an old stump. I kinda liked it. After years of passing it on that path, one day it was gone. The owner of the property had pulled it, filled the hole, and the entrance to the trail seemed kind of empty.

I thought about it for a few days, and finally decided that the owner probably missed the stump just as much as I did, so I gathered 4 of my favorite photographs of it, and wrote a little bit on the back of each, and left them in his mailbox with my business card.

The first pic was of the stump in spring, black with rain, new mushrooms growing around it, a wonderful black and white if I do say so myself.

The second shot was in summer, with Queen Ann's Lace all around it, it made an interesting silhouette against the setting sun.

The third shot was in fall, and the background was brilliant orange and yellow and green, with an adorable chipmunk sitting up top, cheeks puffed full.

The last shot was in winter, the stump appeared black again, partially covered by snow, and out of focus beyond it you knew immediately you were seeing the fuzzy shape of a deer. Adding to the feel there were HUGE snowflakes falling round.

About a week after I left the photos, I got a return letter. It just said: "Thank you. I feel terrible. I thought it was just a stump."

Art is not the product.

It's not the "piece."

Art is the decisions that went into the work,
and nothing else.

-dm

8.

Three students were instructed to photograph a beautiful flower surrounded by stalks of high grass.

The first student rushed out and trampled the grass, to give a clear view to the perfect blossom. He raced to the master and showed him.

"You have captured the flower, but at the expense of its natural surroundings."

Overhearing this, the second student went to his garden and gently pushed apart the stems of grass, and took a clear photograph of the beautiful flower.

He raced to show the Master who said "You too have captured the flower, but was it really all alone in the Universe?"

The third student had paid no attention to the first two, instead walking in slow circles around his garden. Finally, he laid as low as he could on the ground, and shot a picture of the grass.

He took his shot to the Master who looked at it for a long long time.

Finally he said "As beautiful as the flower is, it's natural state made it a mystery. I can see just slivers of it's beauty through the grass in your photo. You have captured not only the flower, but the MYSTERY of the flower as well. This is so much more than a photograph,
it represents......understanding."

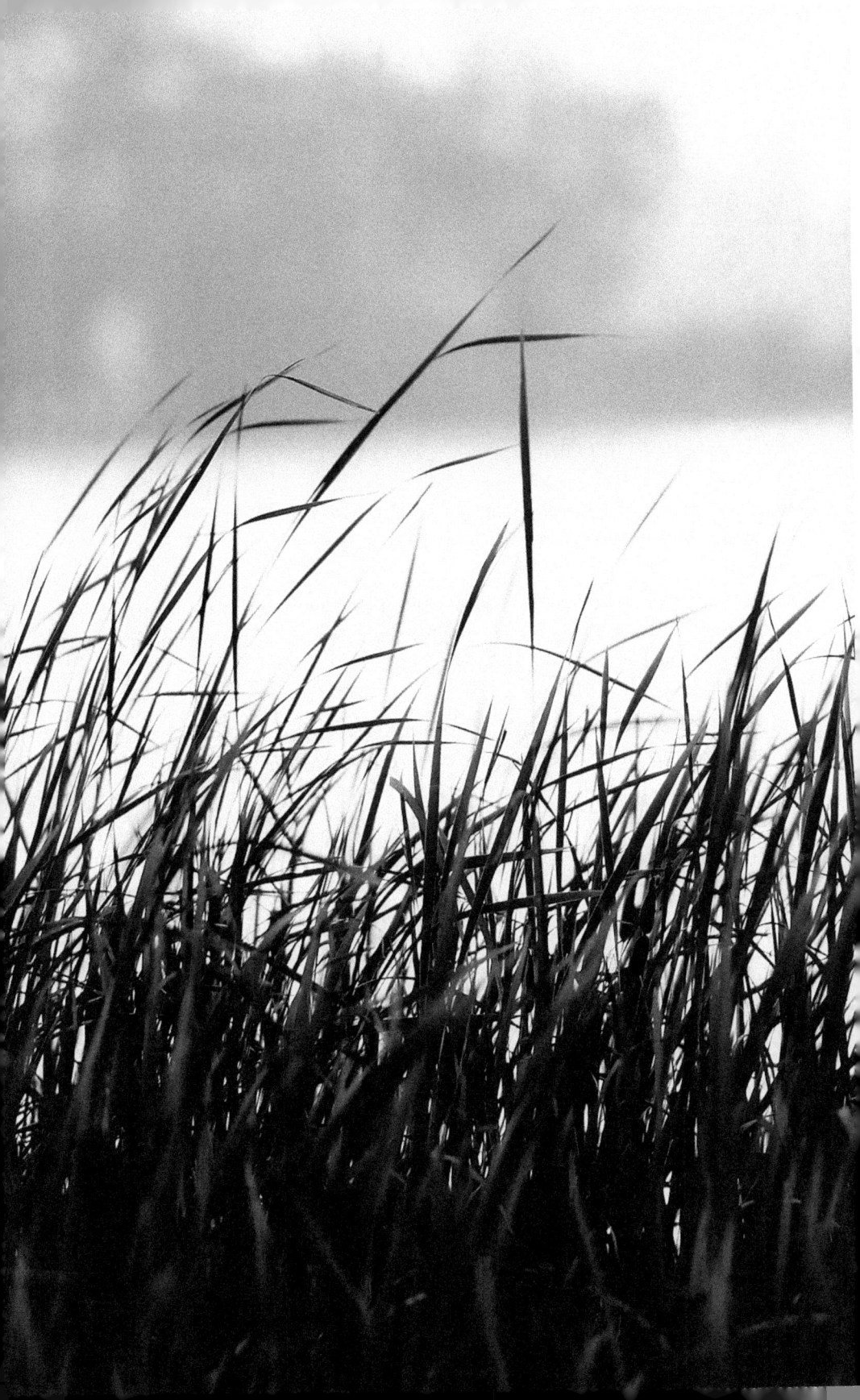

9.

An aspiring artist wanted more than anything to avoid being inspired by others, so he left the city.

But in the country, though sparsely populated, he still found inspiration in the simple inventions and creations of the people.

So he went to the wilderness, and while there were no people, the wilderness itself was a great inspiration, so he secluded himself in a cave, with only a match to provide light.

But when he struck that match, he found he was in awe of the simple pattern in sand at his feet. So he was relieved when that single match burned out.

Until, absent sight, he started noticing the incredible sounds echoing through the cave…

…and wrote a symphony

A single, perfect, diagonal line

is better

than a frame full of disconnected concepts.

10.

The student asked when he would be allowed to move to the next level, and his teacher said "when you can take each idea you've been taught and express it in just one paragraph."

The student thought about that for a very long time, then asked when he would be able to advance to the level above that. The teacher said "when you can take each idea you've been taught and express it in just one sentence."

The student then asked how he would become a master, and the teacher said "I'm assuming it's when you can express each idea that you've learned in just a single word...

...I'll let you know if ever I get there."

11.

The photography instructor took the two students to a small waterfall, spilling into a tiny creek, and said "I want you to think up as many different ways to photograph this waterfall as you can, you have 10 minutes."

Ten minutes later, the first student showed the instructor 5 different photographs...the waterall from the front, the side, the other side, above and just as time was running out, he had taken one from far away.

The instructor then looked to student number two, who had no photographs, only a sheet of paper with this list:

1. From the front, showing symmetry.
2. From the front, subject at 2/3.
3. From the front, portrait orientation, wide angle lens, with an absurd amount of sky.
4. From the side, long lens, shallow depth of field, fast shutter, water drops frozen in time.
5. From the side, wide lens, narrow aperture, slow shutter, water flow motion-blurred to a metallic smooth.
6. From above, straight down with wide lens, showing symmetry.
7. From above, fisheye, waterfall in one corner, winding creek stretching diagonally to the other corner.
8. Panoramic from a distance, narrow aperture, the waterfall tiny in one corner, the sun with visible light rays in the opposite corner.
9. From downstream, wide angle, creek as a subject, waterfall out of focus in the background.
10. Early morning when the light is golden, waterfall backlit by a flash with a blue gel.
11. During heat of the day, infrared, surrounding foliage looking white, cool waterfall looking black.
12. Long exposure at night, flow of the water smooth, stars as a backdrop.
13. From upstream, looking at the point where the waterfall vanishes over the edge, creek out of focus in the background.

...and the student said "I'm sorry, I had more, but I don't write very fast."

99% of everyone

when asked what they want to DO in a photograph,
to make it interesting,

will tell you what they want
in the background instead.

12.

A boy and an old man walked through the forest. After a while, the old man bent and picked up a red stone. "Beautiful" he said. And he carried it.

After a while, he spotted a pearly shell,
and picked it up, said "More beautiful,"
dropping the stone.

After a while, he spotted a blossom, fallen from a tree,
and picked it up. He looked at it, said "More beautiful still,"
and dropped the shell.

After a while, he found a red stone,
very much like the first red stone, and said "Beautiful,"
and dropped the blossom.

The boy looked at him quite puzzled....

And the old man said
"It's always just a matter of mind,
to think that whatever next thing life gives you,

is the most beautiful you've ever seen."

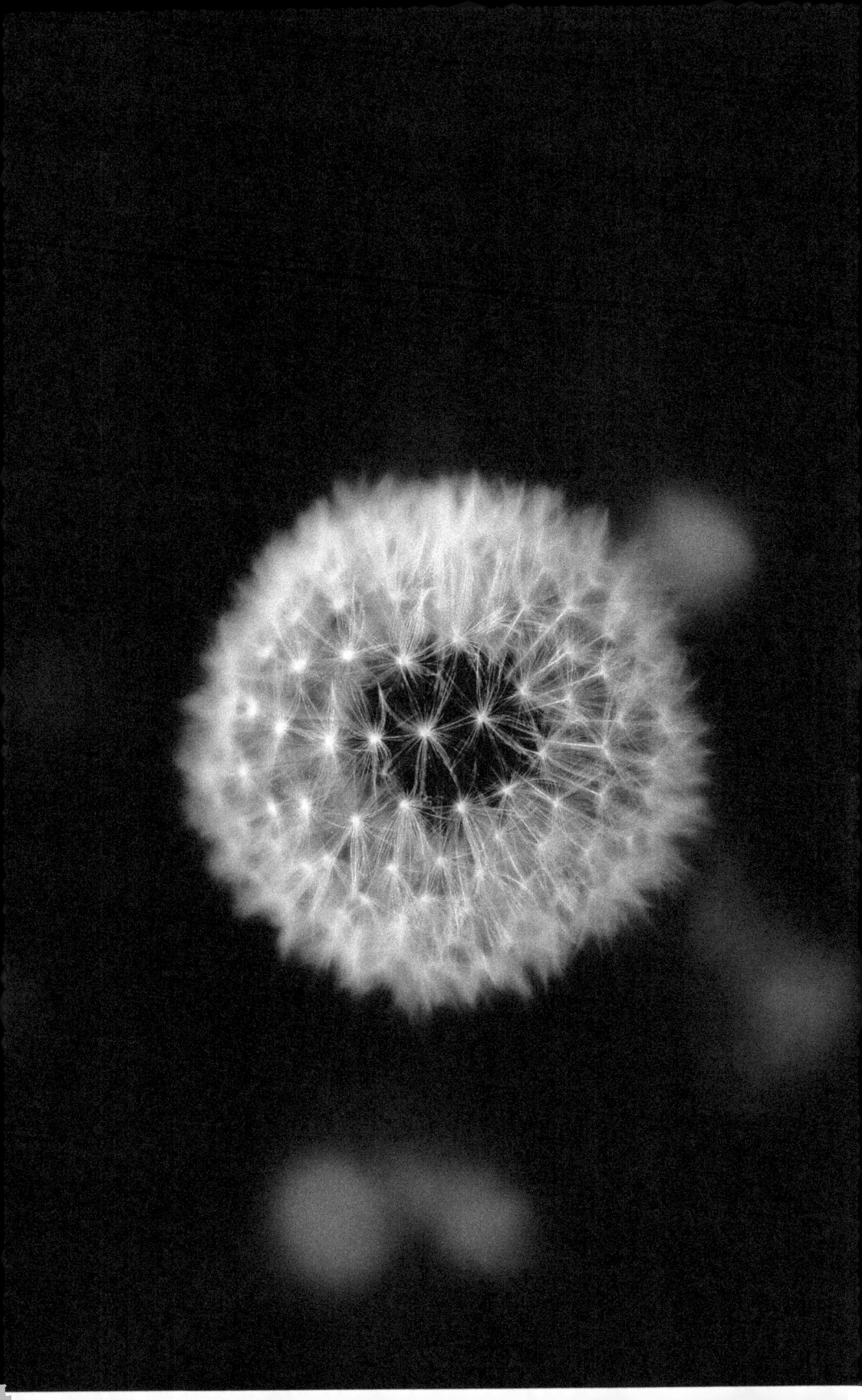

13.

The Master announced that this week's task was to create with "color and composition," and he sent his two students out to create.

At the end of the week, student one came back with a dozen, technically perfect images, and the Master looked at them and nodded, but said "I'll have to ask you to do this task again."

The second student came back with a dozen images that were out of focus…in fact, not just a little out of focus, but dramatically out of focus, and the Master looked at them, shook his head, but said "Yes. You may move on."

The first student was puzzled, and not a little annoyed, asking "Why? HIS images weren't even in focus?"

And the Master replied, "Our assignment this week was color and composition, and he treated those two things as if nothing else in the universe even mattered."

The laws of the Universe limit us all,

save the artist.

-dm

14.

If art were 100% subjective, then everyone would be a great artist.

Not everyone is a great artist.

Therefore, art is not 100% subjective.

If it's not 100% subjective, then it's at least PART objective, meaning it follows rules.

If you want to create art ONLY for yourself, then rules are unimportant.

If on the other hand, one of your goals is to create art that others will appreciate, the only guaranteed way, is to understand the MECHANICS of what makes art...

...good.

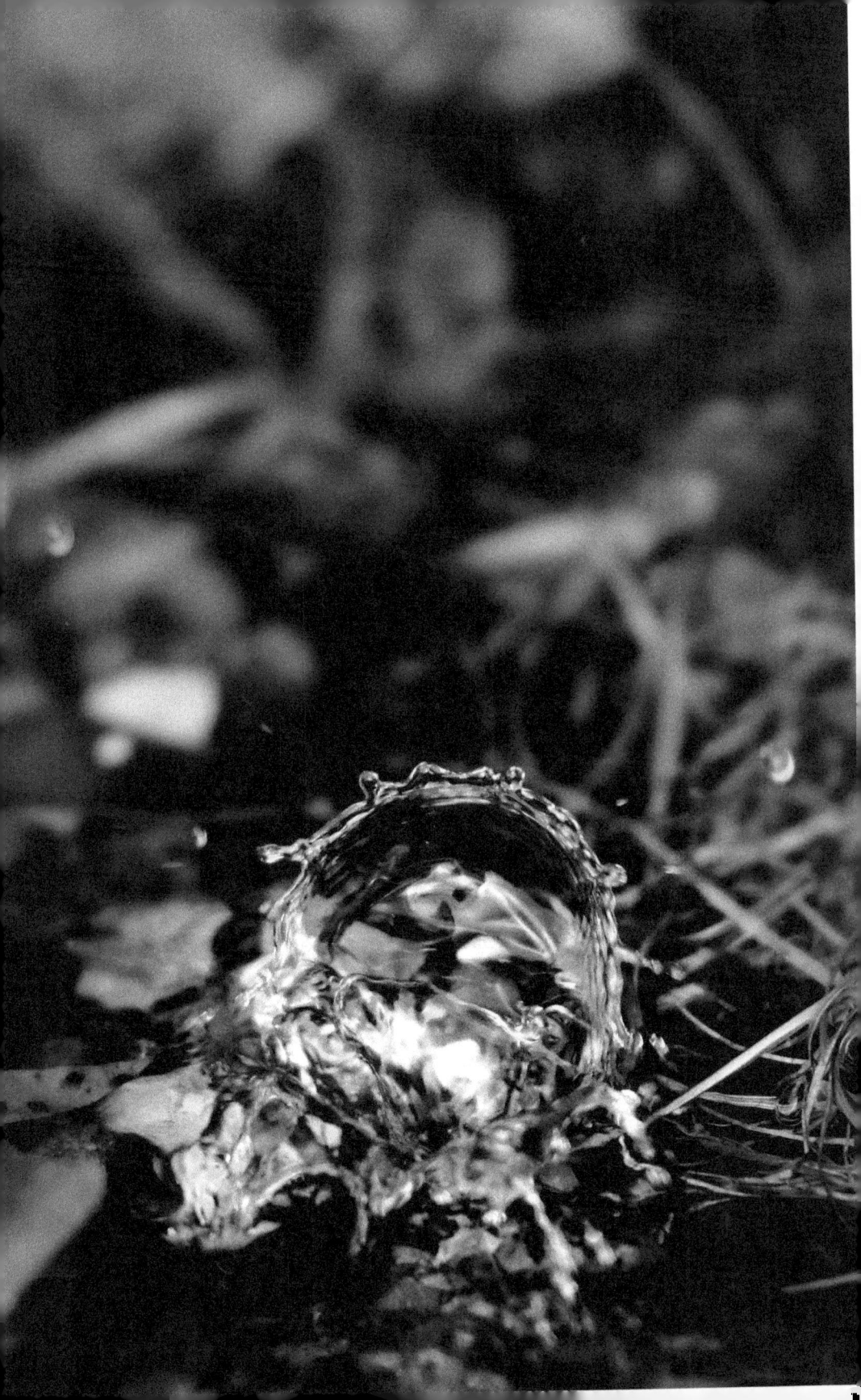

15.

As a challenge for their final year studying photography with the great master, they were tasked with travelling anywhere in the world to capture their final 100 images.

The first student traveled to every continent, to both poles, to the depths of the ocean, to the peaks of mountains. He hiked the rain forest, trekked deserts and floated a hot air balloon over illuminated cities at night. He returned with 100 fabulous photographs, representing all that is beautiful in the world.

Student number two never left home. For one year he photographed only the things he could see from his front door step. At first it was the beautiful...and later it was the interesting, and then finally, the uninteresting and the downright boring. He exhausted everything within sight of his door.

Finished, his folio wasn't nearly as dramatic to look at, but to compensate for a lack of spectacular subjects, it was necessary to be brilliantly clever in style and composition. To make up for not having stunning locations, he had to invent new ways to tell visual stories.

In the end, student one's portfolio was magnificent, but most of the credit went to his subjects, and student two's portfolio was simple, but most of the credit went to the artist.

Any day where I set myself a near-impossible goal,

and chase after it,

is a good day.

-dm

Someone asked me once,

"What makes you a good photographer?"

I answered
"I've seen thousands of great photographs,
and millions of bad one's,

and I knew which were which."

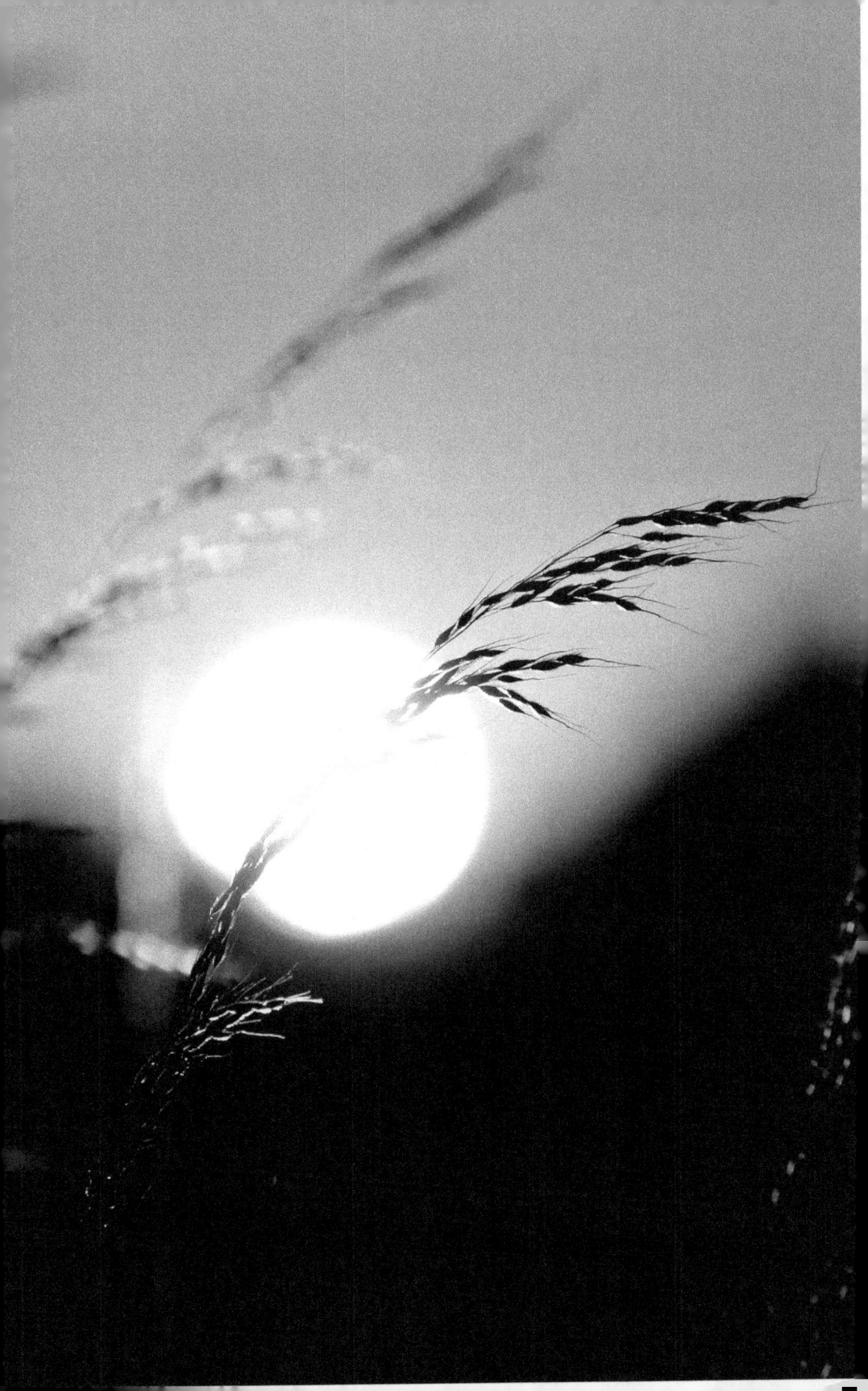

16.

A master sent two students with the task of creating the greatest possible representation of a flower.

The first student positioned the flower just so, surrounded it with flowers that beautifully complimented it, arranged the flowers into a stunning composition, arranged the light to perfectly accent the scene, and then digitally enhanced the color and contrast of the shot to make everything just EXPLODE to the eye.

The second student looked around the flower, lowered himself to the ground and shot from angle where only the flower and a clear sky in the background could be seen.

The master looked at the first student's photography and said "this is a masterwork, you've created an amazing piece of art, exceeding the natural beauty of the original subject in every imaginable way. But you have failed the task."

To the second student he said "And you have passed, for you took every effort to avoid having the photograph be about anything but the subject. You can make a photograph a greater work of art by adding detail, adapting nature, and modifying the results, but it won't make the finished product a better example of the subject itself."

Photography could be described as

The art of recognizing beauty,

And knowing how to isolate it from the rest of the world

And freeze it in time.

-dm

17.

Two students were sent to each study the ways of a tortoise.

The one raced to as close as he could get, but the tortoise hid away in his shell, and the student learned only that tortoises hide in their shell.

The second student stayed as far off as he could, and the tortoise showed him all the things of his nature.

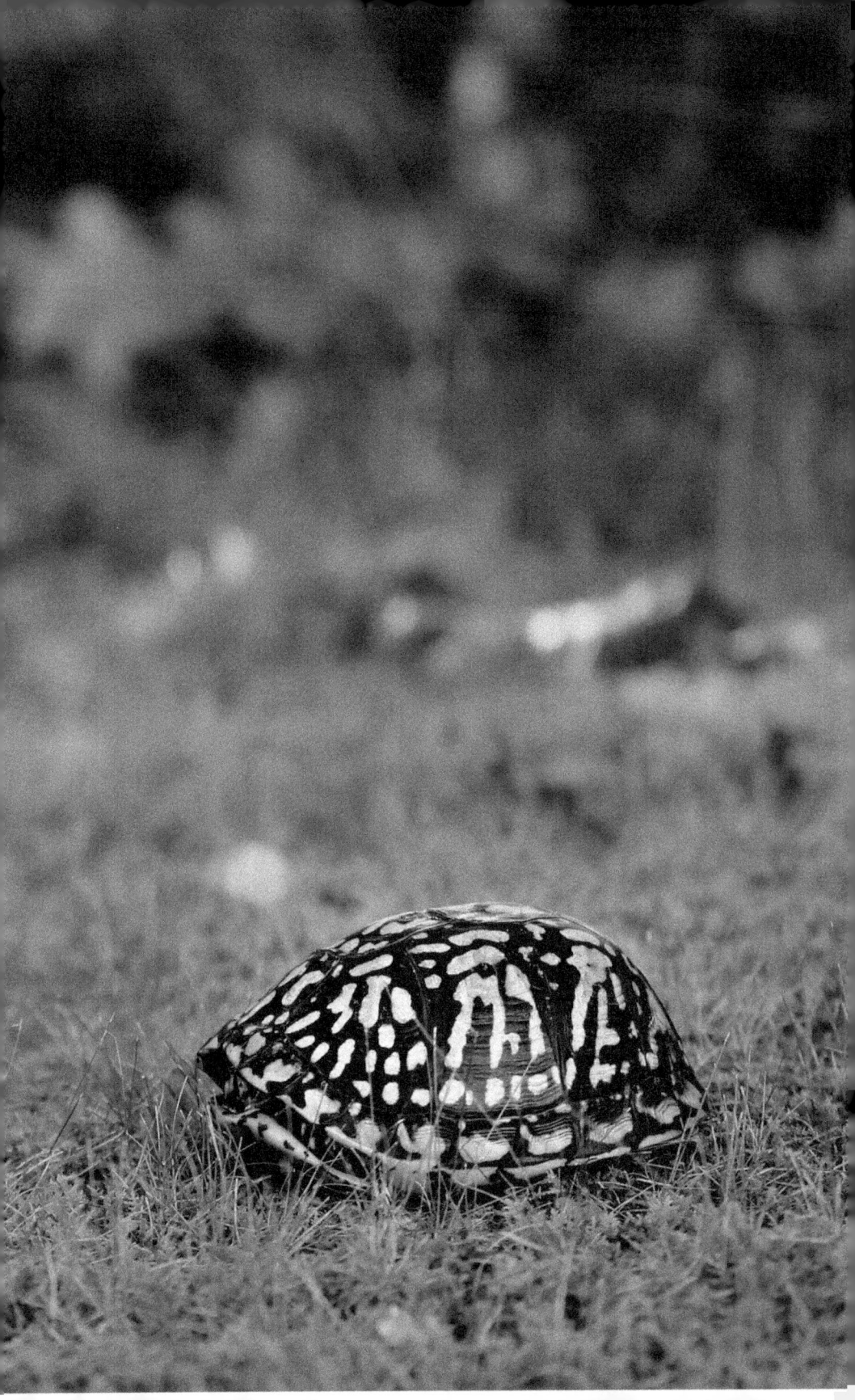

18.

I. I was looking through the online portfolio of one of the world's greatest photographers. Something caught my eye. A photo of a beautiful, ancient painting.

II. I was watching a youth league soccer game one day, and saw a mom working the sidelines with her DSLR pretty hard. Later that night, she posted a picture online and it got RAVE reviews from friends/family/kids......mostly, people said some variation on "GREAT SHOT!"

III. At the end of that same game, I noticed another mom take her son off to one end of the field where she carefully staged a photograph. Later that night, she too posted her pic online, and received praise, but not nearly the level of praise for the first soccer shot.

Three photographs. Three levels of recognition.

continued

The first photograph was seen by, at the very least, thousands, and very likely millions. Virtually everyone that saw it, was impressed. After all, it was not only from a great photographer, it was selected by the great photographer to be among his very best. And the subject was stunning, and fascinating.

The second photograph was seen by, at the very least, hundreds, and possibly thousands. It had praise heaped on it. The shot was action-packed. It had a screaming coach in the background, two kids colliding, both in mid-sprawl toward the ground, and the player at the center of attention was striking the soccer ball with his head, sweat spraying away from the contact, illuminated by the field-lighting behind the player.

The third photograph was seen by dozens, at most hundreds, and those that knew the photographer or the subject liked it, and a few commented with "He looks cute," or "Nice pic."

But the interesting thing I took away from all of this, was that only ONE of those 3 photographs was EXCELLENT.

continued

We use entirely the wrong criteria, in most cases, for evaluating the quality of a photograph. And this misunderstanding leads many, many people to falsely believe they are GOOD photographers. But worse, it keeps them from BECOMING good photographers.

The central concept of this book, is that great photography is about DECISIONS.

Back to our three images. We are often fooled by average photographs of GREAT subjects, and rarely moved by GREAT photographs of average subjects.

Only the third photograph was excellent. That mom put on a wide angle lens, and got at just the right angle and distance from her son to create a dramatic vision. She layed down on the ground to make him taller and more imposing. She focused on him, but recomposed the shot to catch just enough of the scoreboard....not ALL of it, but the bare minimum necessary to know the name of his team and that they won the game. She didn't have the child standing in front of the scoreboard, with the scoreboard perpendicular to the shot, but instead it was askew, creating a strong diagonal in the finished image. That mom sacrificed some pure image quality, gaining an edgy grain, by turning up her ISO setting. That was necessary because she had narrowed her aperture to make sure the player and the scoreboard AND the stadium lights were all in focus, and the narrow aperture made the lights look like starbursts. After she set up her composition, she had her son race up and kick the ball past her, and in just one shot (as best I could tell from watching) she captured a perfect photograph.

She made a LOT of decisions. Her shot was art.

continued

Why didn't the other mom's photograph fit that category? In a method quite different from above, she put her camera on auto-exposure. Auto white balance. Auto ISO. She shot the action, the center of the action, non-stop for 2 hours, clicking off probably 2000 frames. Sometimes the action was interesting, sometimes it wasn't, and ONCE, more or less by luck, several things happened at the same time, in the same frame, and made HER look GREAT. But the only decision she made, was to follow the ball, and keep clicking.

Why wasn't the photograph from the famous photographer great? His portfolio was loaded, for sure, with many many beautiful, fascinating, AMAZING images. And this image was quite amazing. But it was a shot of another person's artwork. The artwork filled the frame completely, so there was no composition from the photographer. The lighting was even and natural, so there was no lighting DECISION by the photographer. In fact, the only decision the photographer apparently made, was WHAT to shoot. But he was assigned to be there, and everyone who went there would have taken a picture of that artwork. Most with a point and shoot camera on auto-everything that would have yielded pretty much the same photo.

Now you could argue that it was the job of that professional photographer to capture a perfect image of that artwork, exactly as he had, which is probably true. But great photography is about decisions, and he didn't really make any in the capturing of that photo. And what really made me think about that shot, was the photographer's decision to include it among his best. After all, there was almost nothing in that photograph that was HIS to claim.

Great photography is about making decisions. The fact is, anyone with a modern smartphone can make a great image of the Grand Canyon at sunset.   But if you take away the VALUE of the SUBJECT by itself, you start to see the parts of the photograph the ARTIST can really take credit for.

If you put a truly excellent photographic artist on location, surrounded by boring subjects, he should still come away with amazing photographs.

This book is about thinking of GREAT photography in a different way. It's about realizing that YOU have to make decisions or it's not YOUR image to claim. It's about becoming good at something, not by repeating what others have done, but by CREATING on your own.

Most people want to take great photographs, and traditional education has us believing that that can be taught. I believe that teaching someone DEPRIVES them of the chance to be great, so this book is about learning the PHILOSOPHY OF...the ART OF....PHOTOGRAPHY.

So that you can set this book down and make your own path.

fini

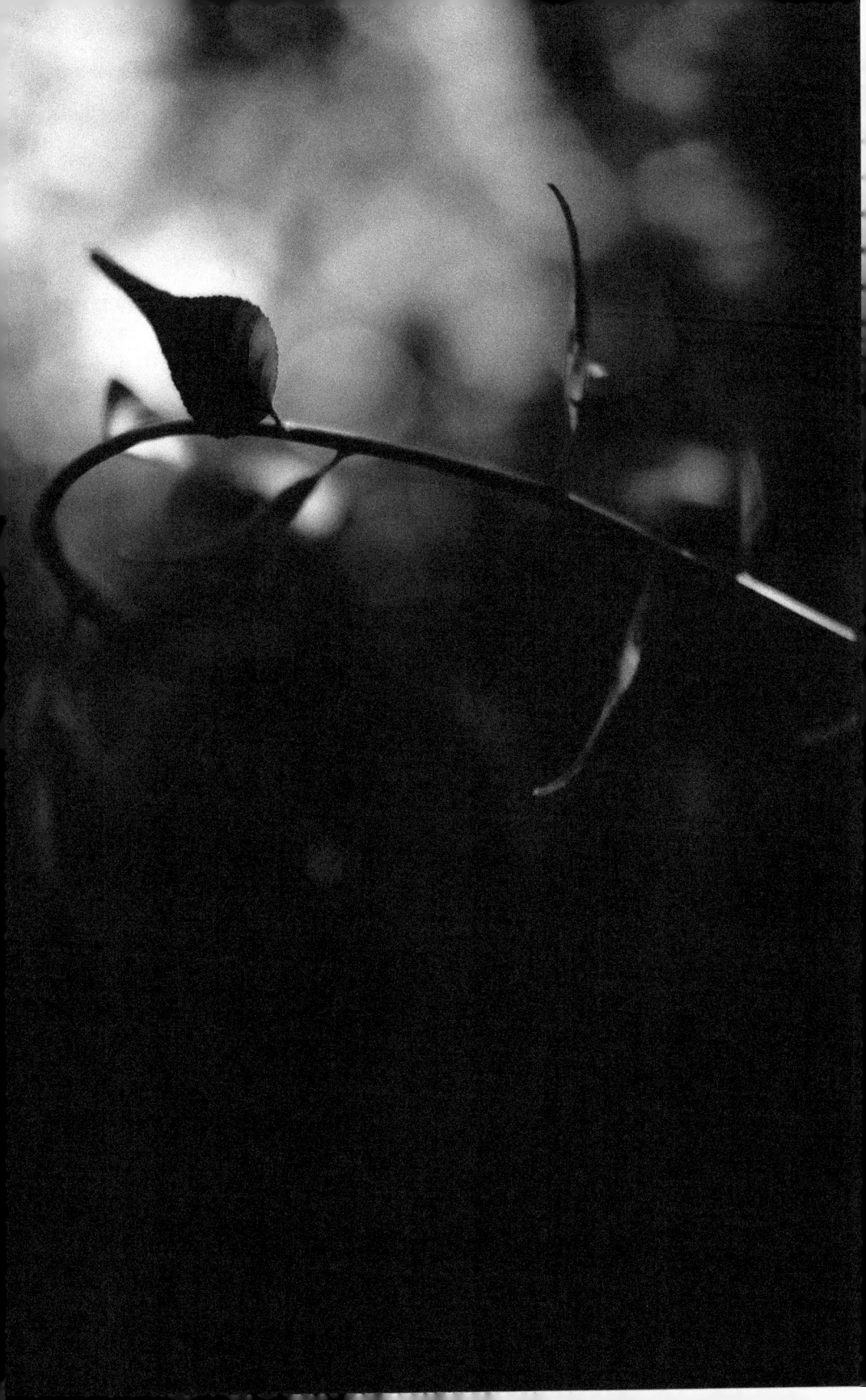

19.

The master asked the student: "What in this clearing is the most interesting suject?" The student immediately pointed out the brilliant red tree across the way, in front of a brilliant blue sky. The Master said "Yes, quite beautiful, now go sit down with your back against it."

Next the Master asked "Now, what remains as the most interesting subject?" Unable to see the tree in it's glory, he chose instead a patch of amazing yellow flowers, extended on long green stems. The Master said "Yes, quite beautiful, now rotate around to the opposite side of the tree you're sitting against."

Next the Master again asked "NOW, what remains as the most interesting subject...." And object by object the Master continued to eliminate the 20 most interesting subjects from the view of the student."

The student was puzzled, there was nothing left for him to photograph. The Master then said "Now sit there, for however long it takes, for you to compose and capture something interesting."

The student was frustrated, and hours passed....but when he was no longer allowed to consider the red tree, or the yellow flowers, or ANY of the other obviously interesting subjects in the clearing...he began to notice....the ants. The sticks. The pebbles. He saw clouds forming shapes and scrub brush that would look great in black and white.

In the end he took many amazing photographs he never would have otherwise seen.

I finally have an answer for one of the most annoying questions a photographer ever gets.

After seeing a particularly impressive photograph you've taken, someone asks "wow, that's amazing, what camera did you use?"

….as if suggesting that great pictures come from having the right camera.

From now on when someone says "Wow, that's amazing, what camera did you use"

I'll say "Mine."

20.

She sent me a link to an album and said
"Take a look at my pics, and tell me what you think!"

I said "They're all of you..."

She said "Yeah, is that bad?"

I said "No, but tell me...what part of YOU are you MOST insecure about?"

It took some persuading but she finally said "My legs."

I said "What part of your body are you most confident about?"

She said "My eyes."

I said "How many pictures in that album are of your eyes?"

She said "Ummm, most of 'em."

"How many are of your legs?"

"Ummmmmm, none of them."

"You don't need me to evaluate your skill as a photographer..."

"Why not?"

"Because even you don't think you're any good."

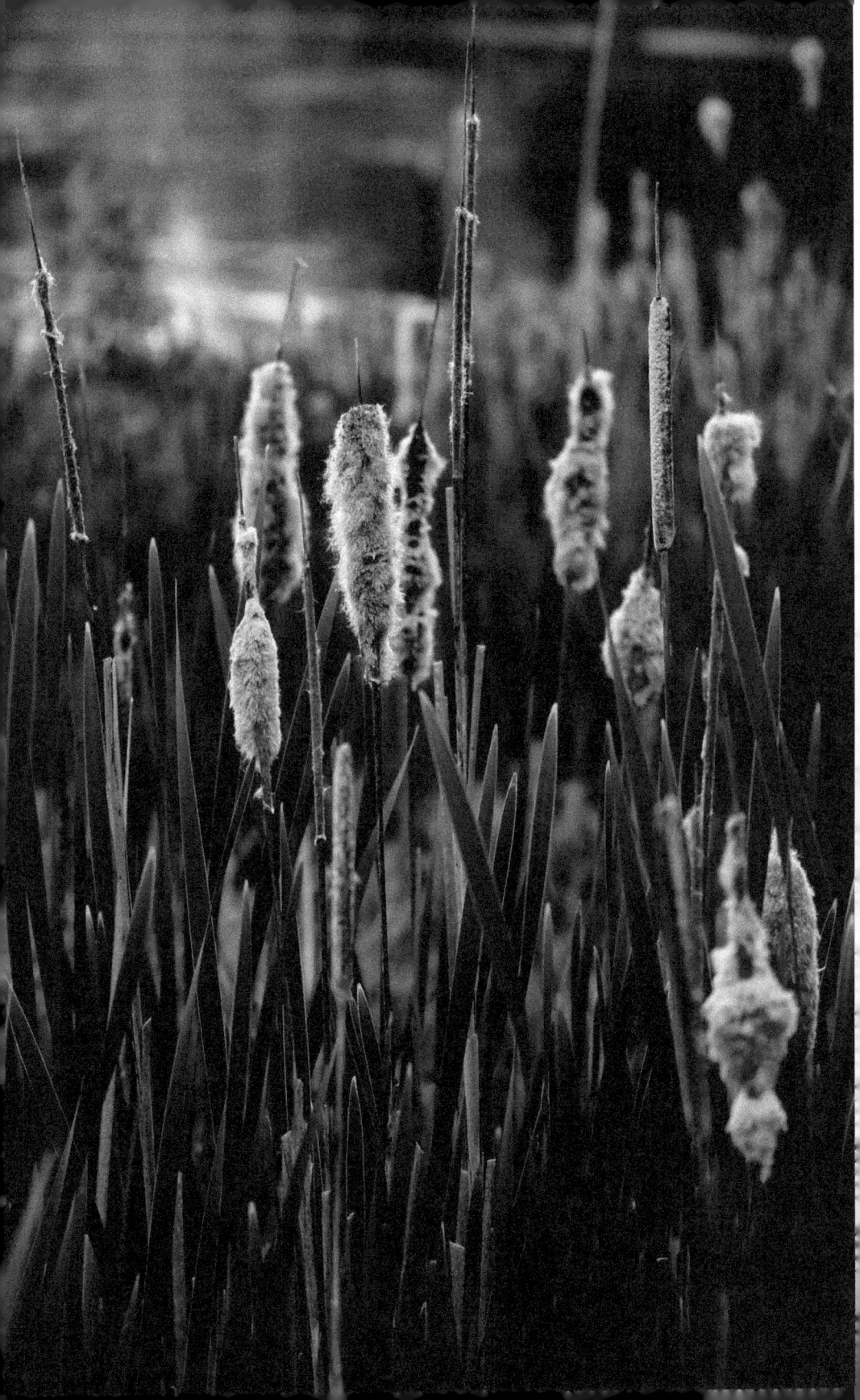

21.

And finally they came to the test on photo-editing, and the Master put before each student a photo of a statue at the end of the pier, behind the school. It was too dark, the colors were wrong, there was an empty pack of cigarettes laying next to the beautiful statue….the photo was a mess, a lot to fix.

He told them all they have one day.

The next day all three students presented their edited images…..the master looked at the first student's and said "Very nice, you've corrected the light, and the color, and removed that ugly trash…but it feels, kind of……….fake."

He looked at student number two's and said "You've taken this beyond fixing, the sky in the background is brilliant blue, the dock appears even more weathered, everything has been fixed. But, it feels……………….. edited."

Then he looked at student number three's and was amazed!

"This is FABULOUS! The sky is incredible, the problems are gone, everything is not only corrected but improved!
And it all feels so NATURAL! Tell us about your techniques…"

And the student said, "Well first…………….I went out back and took a better picture."

Circles are only perfect in theory...

...in practice they are utterly impossible.

-dm

The Fives.

Go out shooting for 2 hours, take only 5 photos...
...no deleting, no reviewing

Go out shooting and take a single shot each,
of 5 dramatically different subjects

Go out shooting and shoot only ONE subject,
but create 5 dramatically different interpretations.

Go out shooting, and shoot as many different subjects
as you can in just 5 minutes.

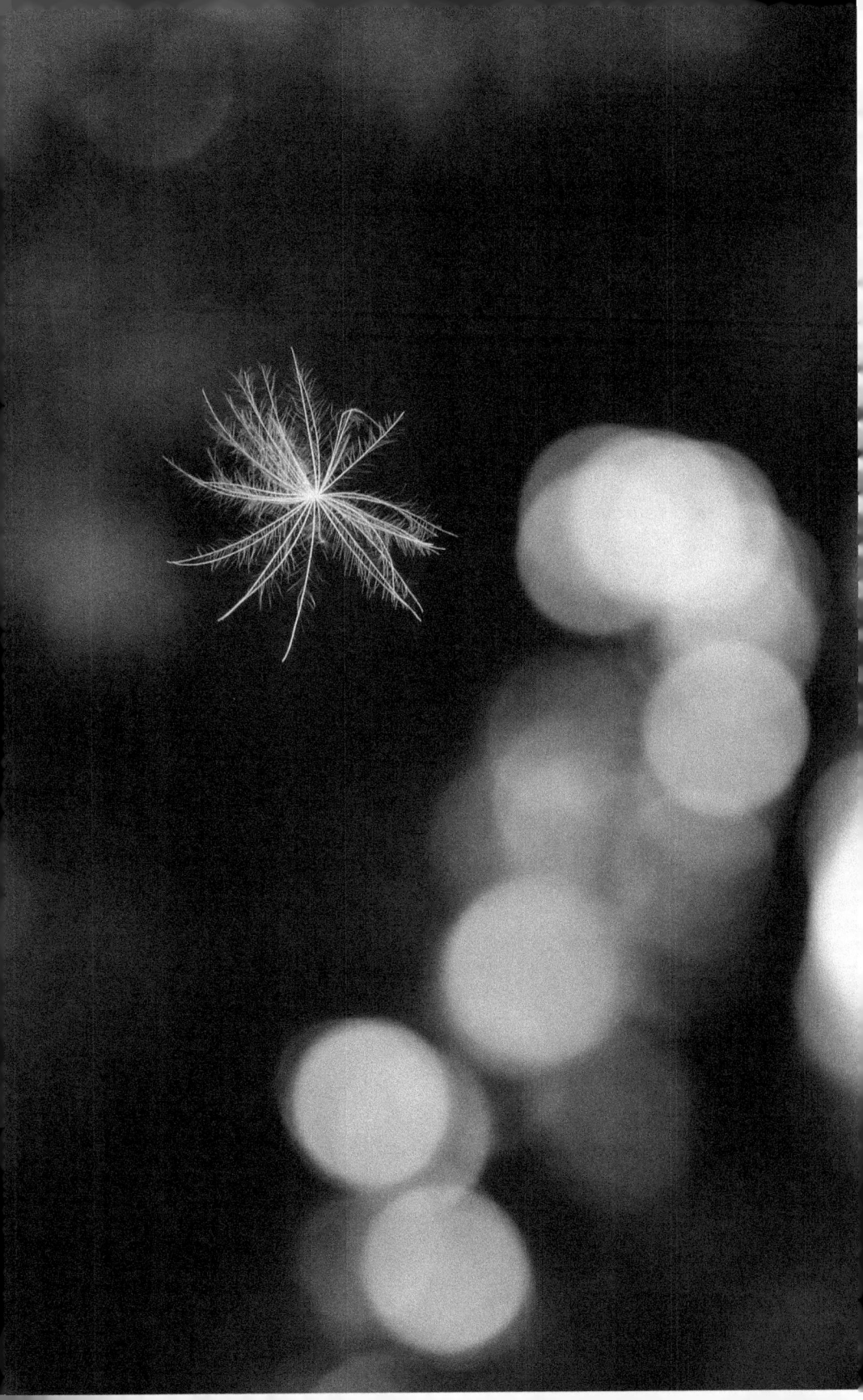

Most people design a photograph by adding more and more...

...it's often best to start with a scene

and remove everything not necessary to the composition.

If you let the camera make the decisions,

you're not a photographer, your a tripod.

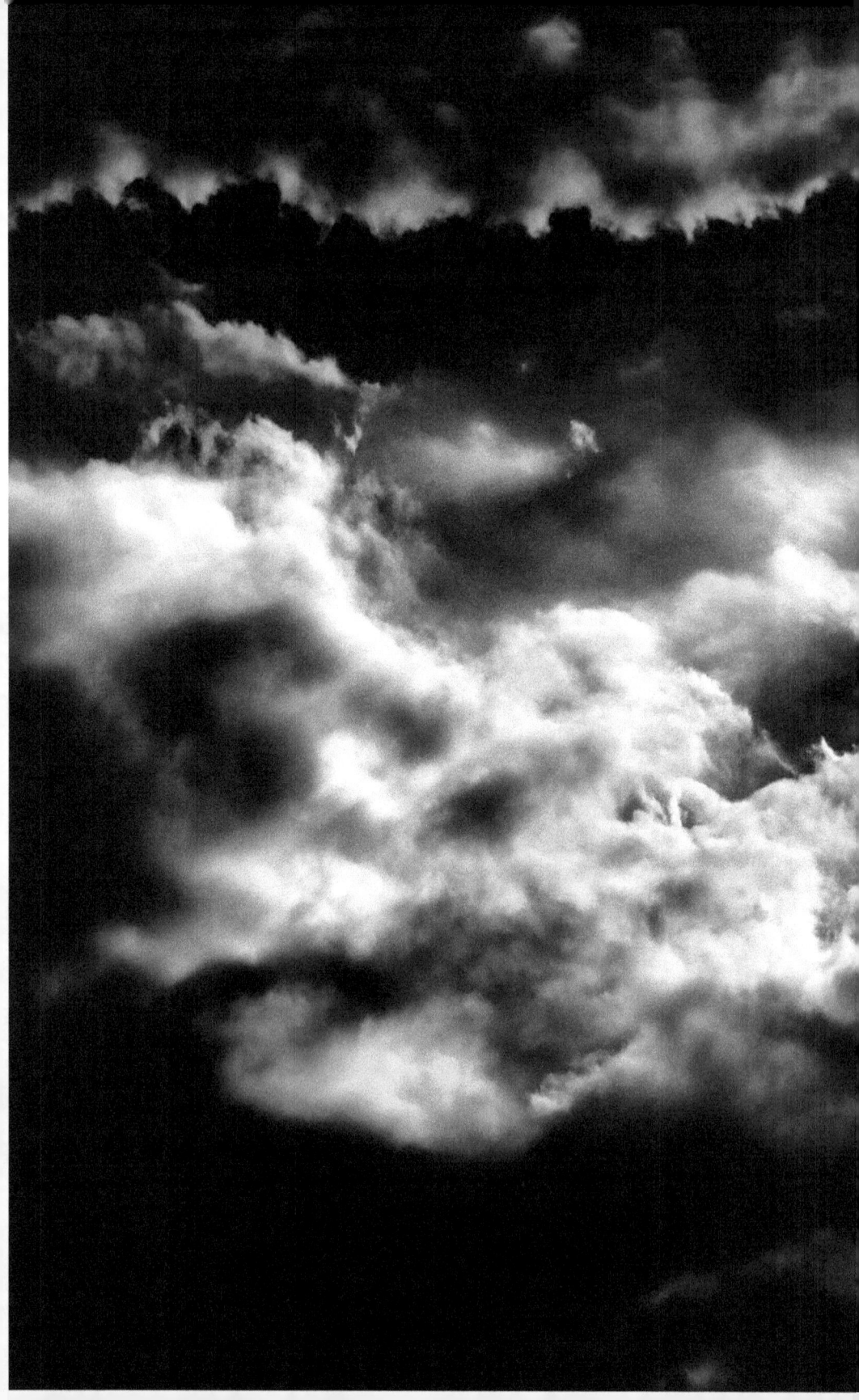

The amount of art created grows,
the amount of art not yet created never changes.

22.

After weeks of training, the master throws open the doors to the room containing every piece of photography equipment ever......and tells the two students to choose whatever they need to spend a day GUARANTEEED to improve them as photographers.

One student chooses everything he can carry.
The other chooses the simplest camera with no additional equipment.

Later that night, student one returns, proudly displaying an array of photographs he was never able to take before...

...and student number two returned with a much more modest product, but with an array of skills he had acquired in overcoming the limitations of his gear.

If you have a great passion for something,

don't analyze it.

-dm

When you have an original idea, you run the risk of being laughed at.

When you have a GOOD original idea,
you run the risk of being followed,
with the pressure that comes with leadership.

When you have a GREAT idea,
the risk is that you won't speak up,
for fear of being followed or laughed at.

-dm

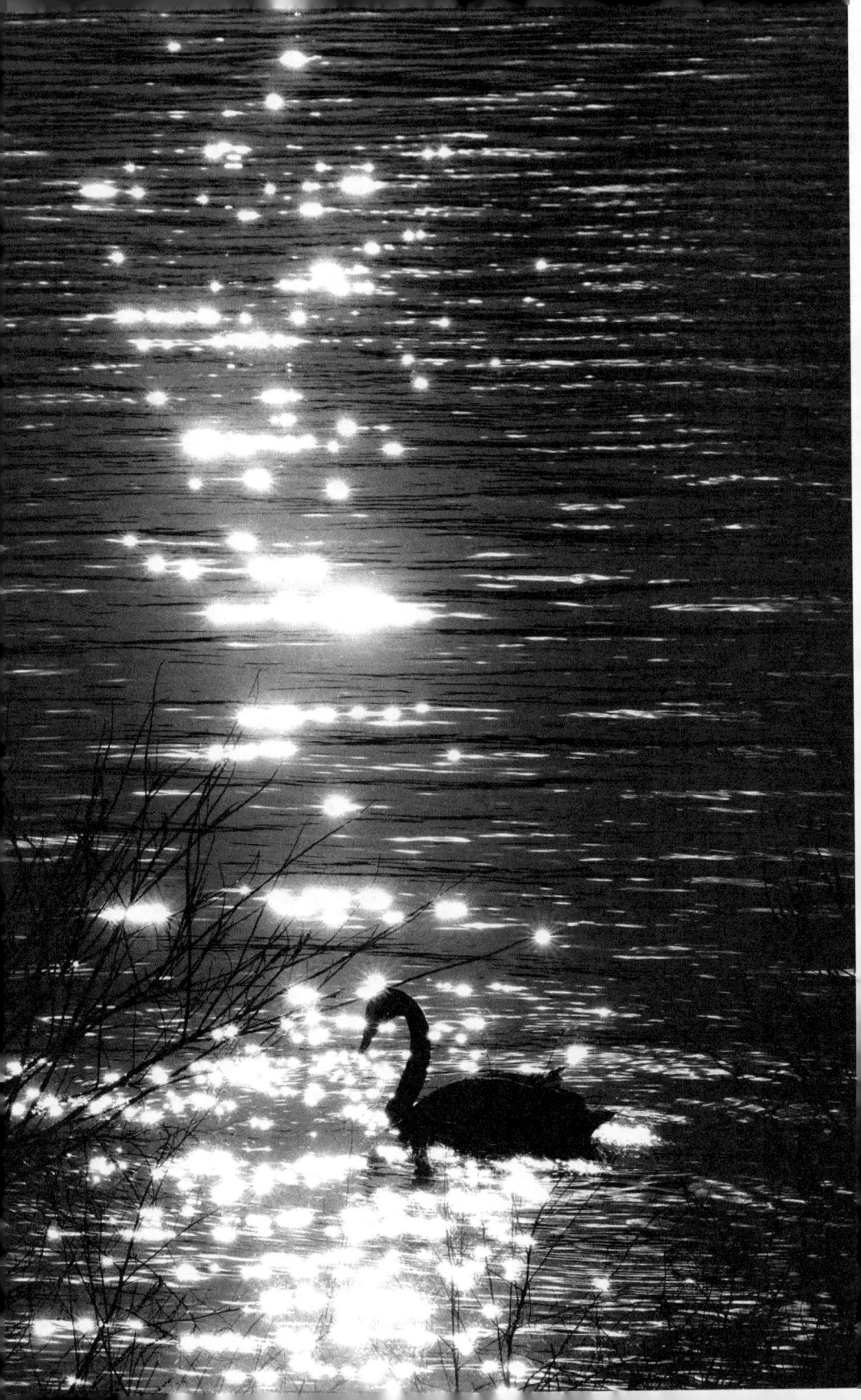

23.

The instructor sent his 10 best students, one at a time, all on the same assignment. Their direction is to photograph a flower, that grows at the edge of the marshland.

After, the instructor asks student one what makes his photograph interesting, and the student replies that it's the setting sun in the background.

The instructor asks student two, and the response is "I shot from straight above, so the flower would have a symetric geometry.

And the instructor continues through all of the students, until the last, who he's surprised to see is covered head to toe in thick, black mud.

Heooks at the student's photograph and says "To me, nothing in particular stands out about this, can you tell me what it is that makes yours interesting?

And the student replied "I just kind of thought that if I held the camera way over my head, and waded into the swamp to my nose, I'd get a shot that no one else had.

I'm a scientist by nature,

but I can't help but wonder,

just how amazing the world would have been,

before we knew how any of it worked.

-dm

One of the photographer's most potent tools....
...a fascination with the simplest of things.

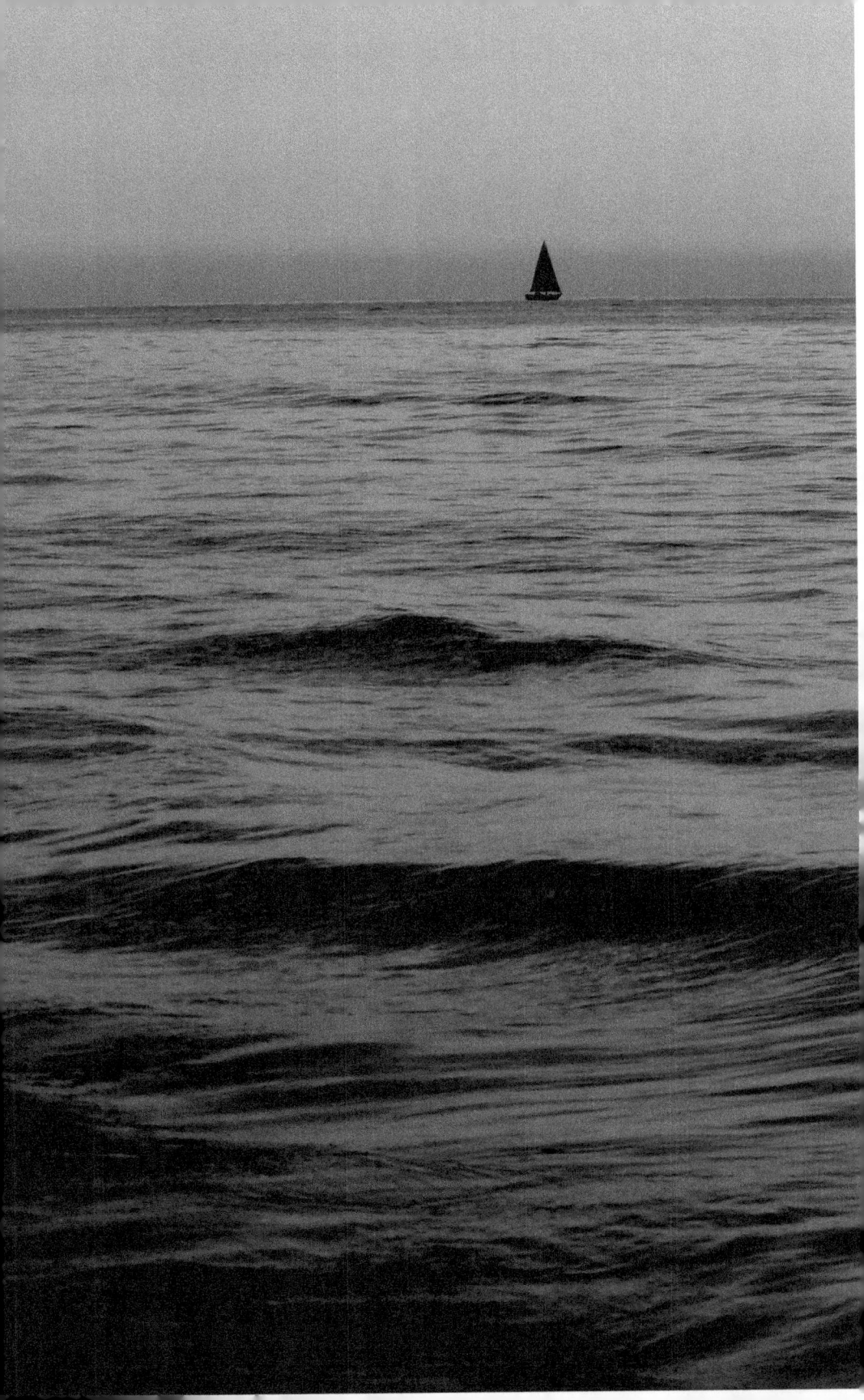

24.

And having studied with all the great photography masters, he finally came to his last test.

The final master, the wisest of the great photographers, gave him 5 days, to list every single feature, or technique, or style, or subject, or concept, or element that could contribute to an excellent photograph.   It was quite a task, even given plenty of time….to think, to remember virtually everything he'd been taught, and to put all of it down on paper.

He worked tirelessly for 5 days and even some nights, and listed every single thing he could think of. He returned to the master who examined it for quite some time. It was page after page after page of every single thing the student could think of, that could be used to create a work of photographic art.

Finally, the master said "You have done very well. You have learned a great deal, and you have done a wonderful job of listing EVERYthing, every tool of creation you might use to make a beautiful photograph……but I will give you one last chance to add to the list, is there ANYthing else?"

Worried that the master was looking for something specific, something he had left off his list, his mind raced 'round desperately trying to think of it. The master was supernaturally patient, as one hour, then two, then three hours went by.

Finally the student said "No, I believe the list is complete."

A large smile spread across the master's face, and the student relaxed, started breathing again, and smiled himself…

…and the Master said "Now go take a photograph without using anything on this list."

A lot of people claim they're not creative...

I think that much of the time

it's not a failure to create,

but a fear of sharing the idea that trips people up.

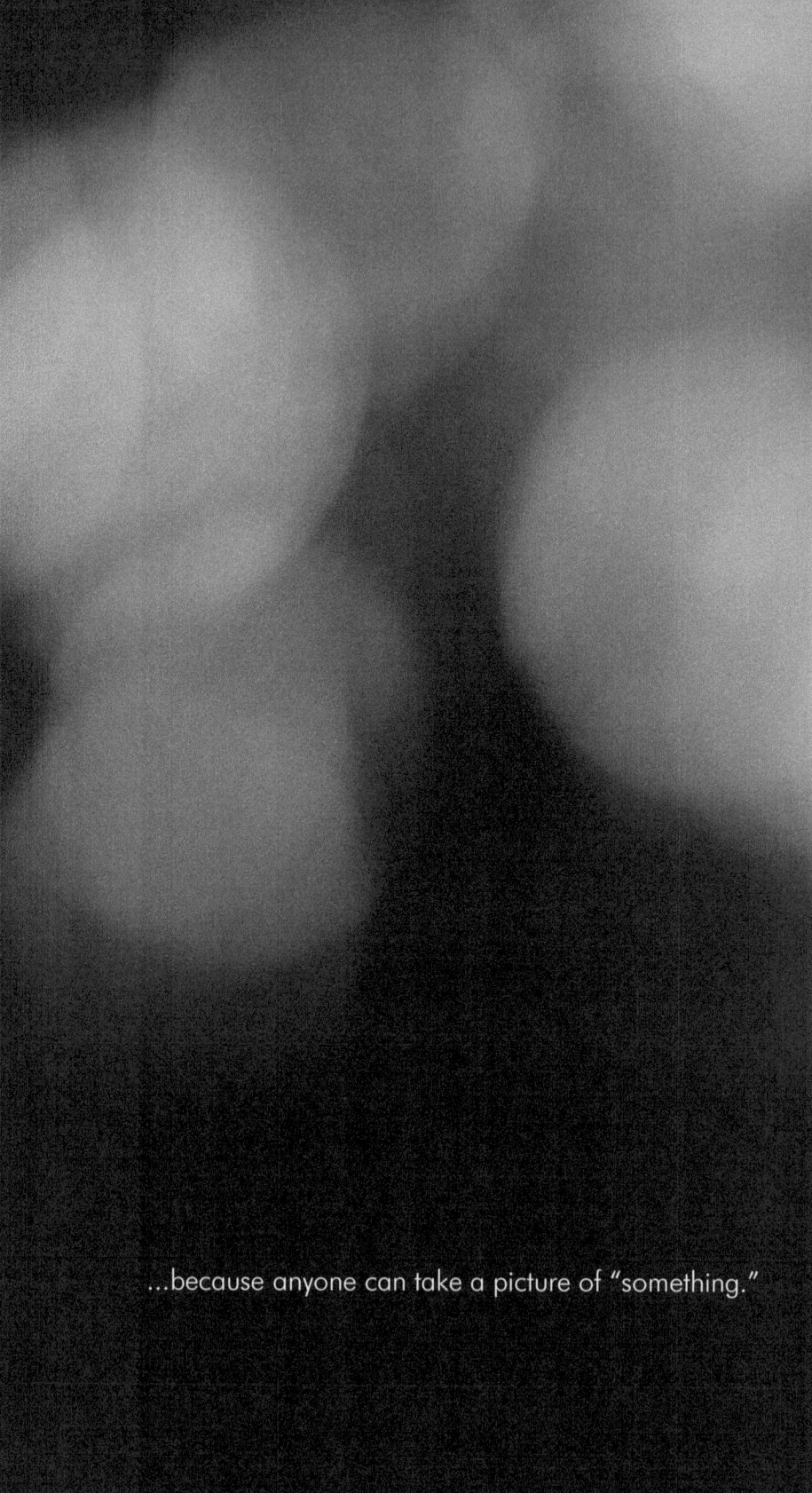

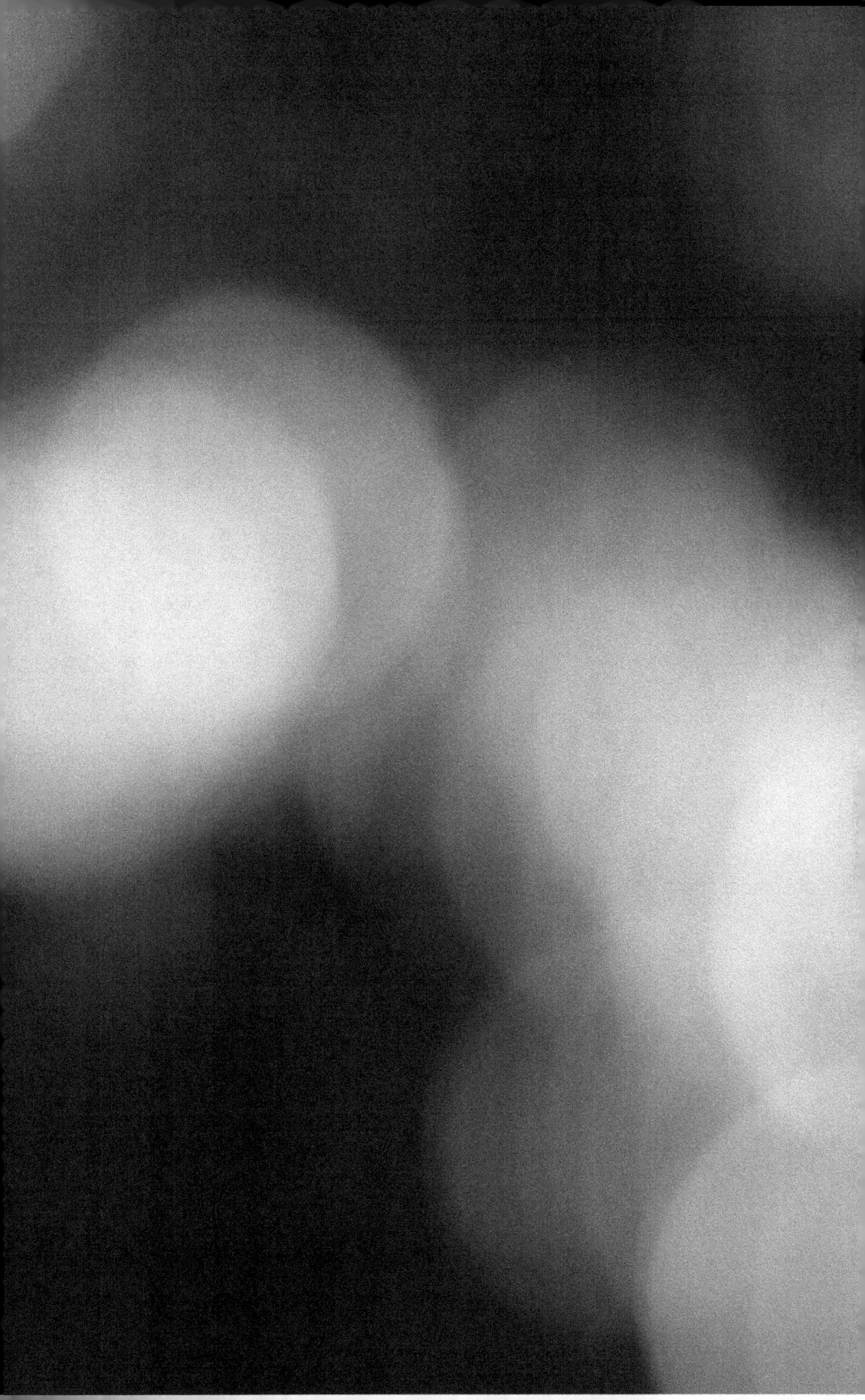

The Mountain and the Pebble

There is no higher honor, than being asked to "photograph The Mountain."

Only two students each year are invited. Each is tasked with capturing a single, magnificent photo of the most visually striking subject in the land.....The Mountain.

Looking at the image from the first student for a whole day, the great Photographer-Philospher finally announces that the shot is beautiful. Brilliant color, detail, contrast, style and composition. A truly fine work. He said "You have learned well."

But the photograph from the second student was a different matter, and challenged the Master.

He examined it for a whole day....and then another....and then a third.

Finally calling both students to him, he repeated that the first photograph had been quite a work of technical skill, but that the second student had accomplished something on an entirely different level, and would be replacing him, as Master.

For years and years, he had evaluated the students' images of The Mountain, and in all that time, something had never occurred to him.

Photographing The Mountain was easy. The subject was spectacular in every way.

And the second student had figured this out, and found a way to rise well above the challenge.

In his image, The Mountain was only a shape...an out of focus blur in the background, and in the foreground, a lowly pebble.

But the student had gone to great lengths to find the perfect pebble, in the perfect spot, and had reasoned out his shot in every detail.

He had gotten right down next to the ground, and shot with just the right lens, at just the right angle, with just the right light....to make the pebble look like a mountain.

The old Master said "You see....anyone can make a magnificent mountain, look like a magnificent mountain. Only a true artist can make a mountain from just a pebble."

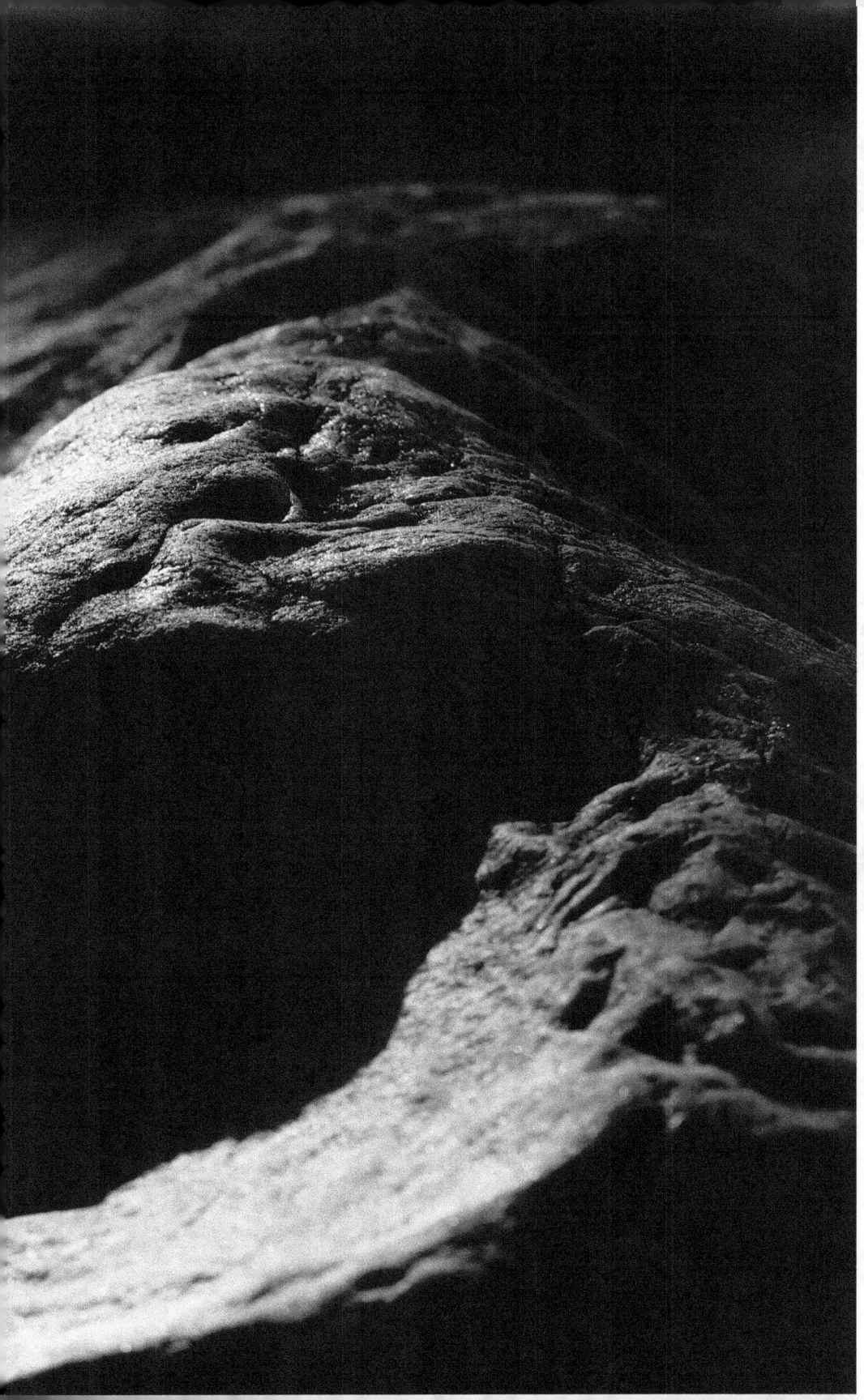

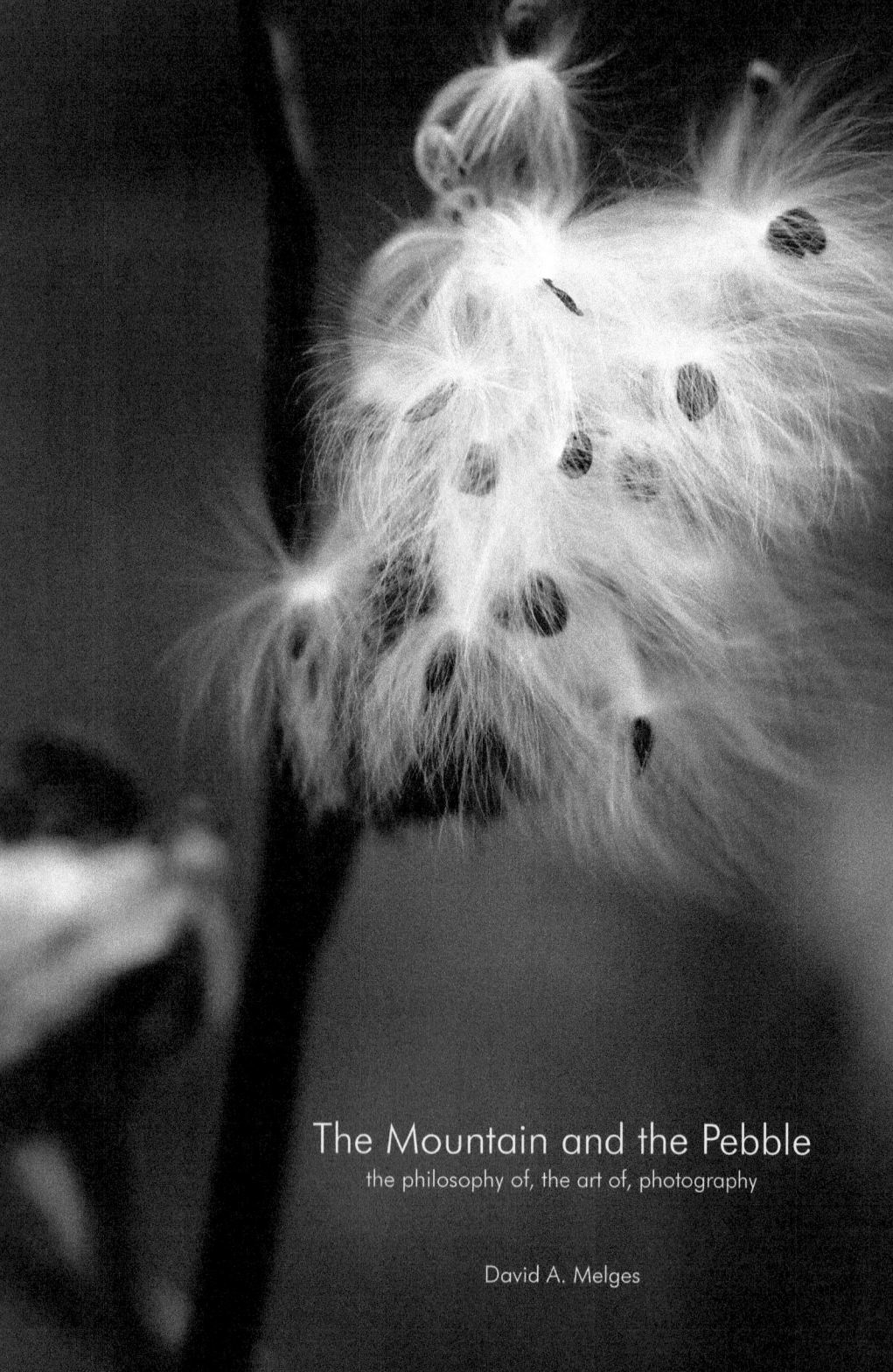

The Mountain and the Pebble
the philosophy of, the art of, photography

David A. Melges

The Wrap-Up

This project started in 2002. It was then that a light went on...

I took a picture of a rose, and showed it around with great pride. I thought of it as a great picture, but everyone that looked at the shot, commented on the beauty of the rose.

"That rose is GORGEOUS!"
"That's the most INCREDIBLE red rose!"

It suddenly hit me that they were right, the subject was wonderful, the photo itself was just a snapshot.

So I started taking pictures of roses all the time, and working out new and creative ways to capture them.

One winter's day, I took another single red rose outside, and misted it with water until it was covered in a sheen of glassy ice. I found the perfect location where setting sunlight would come through the ice, but the background would be a deep, dark blue.

I was shooting with a camera that had naturally deep depth of field, so I was also careful to pick a spot where the distance between my subject and that dark background was very great.

And I waited.

7 hours.

Until the light was perfect.

The first person who saw the photograph said "That is the best PICTURE of a rose I've ever seen.

And my experiment was complete. I'd proven to myself that what makes a great photograph is not the subject, but the choice of the subject...and all the decisions that lead to the quality of the finished image.

It's about DECISIONS.

Copyright © 2013 David A. Melges
All rights reserved.
ISBN: 1493759523
ISBN-13: 978-1493759521

www.ingramcontent.com/pod-product-compliance
Lightning Source LLC
Chambersburg PA
CBHW051817170526
45167CB00005B/2047